# VECTORS

## APHORISMS & TEN-SECOND ESSAYS

*James Richardson*

AUSABLE PRESS
2001

Design and composition by Ausable Press.
The type faces are Trajan and Dante.
Cover design by Rebecca Soderholm.

Published by
AUSABLE PRESS
46 EAST HILL ROAD
KEENE NY 12942

www.ausablepress.com

The Acknowledgements appear on page 109 and
constitute a continuation of the copyrights page.

LIBRARY OF CONGRESS CATALOGING-IN-PUBLICATION DATA
Richardson, James, 1950—
  Vectors : aphorisms & ten-second essays / James Richardson.— 1st ed.
    p. cm.
  ISBN 0-96772668-8-2 (alk. paper)— ISBN 0-9672668-9-0 (pbk. : alk. paper)
    1. Aphorisms and apothegms. I. Title.
PS3568.I3178 V43 2001
818'.5402—dc21                                              2001045903

For Connie, more than ever.

ALSO BY JAMES RICHARDSON

*How Things Are* (2000)
*A Suite for Lucretians* (1999)
*As If* (1992)
*Vanishing Lives: Tennyson, D.G. Rossetti, Swinburne,
and Yeats* (1988)
*Second Guesses (1984)*
*Thomas Hardy: The Poetry of Necessity* (1977)
*Reservations* (1977)

1.

The road reaches every place, the short cut only one.

2.

Those who demand consideration for their sacrifices were making investments, not sacrifices.

3.

What you give to a thief is stolen.

4.

Despair says *I cannot lift that weight.* Happiness says, *I do not have to.*

5.

You've never said anything as stupid as what people thought you said.

6.

Our avocations bring us the purest joys. Praise my salads or my softball, and I am deified for a day. But tell me I am a great teacher or a great writer and you force me to tell myself the truth.

7.

Ah, what can fill the heart?  But then, what *can't?*

8.

Shadows are harshest when there is only one lamp.

9.

Desire's most seductive promise is not pleasure but change, not that you might possess your object but that you might become the one who belongs with it.

10.

I say nothing works any more, but I get up and it's tomorrow.

11.

A beginning ends what an end begins.

12.

I walk up the drive for the morning paper and find myself musing, as if the news were fiction, *Marvelous that they think of all this, so deadpan strange.* Nothing is so improbable as the truth. If the day's headlines hadn't already happened, they would not happen.

13.

Gravity's reciprocal: the planet rises to the sparrow's landing.

14.

When a jet flies low overhead, every glass in the cupboard sings. Feelings are like that: choral, not single; mixed, never pure. The sentimentalist may want to deny the sadness or boredom in his happiness, or the freedom that lightens even the worst loss. The moralist will resist his faint complicity. The sophisticate, dreading to be found naive, will exclaim upon the traces of vanity or lust in any motive, as if they were the whole. Each is selling himself simplicity; each is weakened with his fear of weakness.

15.

Road: what the man of two minds travels between them.

16.

The cynic suffers the form of faith without its love. Incredulity is his piety.

17.

Pessimists live in fear of their hope, optimists in fear of their fear.

18.

Writer: how books read each other.

19.

Some people live in a continual state of skepticism and annoyance that they cultivate as a kind of worldly wisdom and are always recruiting for. Let the sun come up and they will roll their eyes, *Wouldn't you know it?* Profess to be content and they will be disappointed that you have sold your soul for trifles. They wait, hurt and righteous, for the world to prove it really loves them.

20.
If the couple could see themselves twenty years later, they might not recognize their love, but they would recognize their argument.

21.
Each lock makes two prisons.

22.
Painting high on the house. Yellow jackets swarmed around me. I couldn't convince them I was harmless, so I had to kill them.

23.
All stones are broken stones.

24.
Of all the ways to avoid living, perfect discipline is the most admired.

25.
Why would we write if we'd already heard what we wanted to hear?

26.
It is by now proverbial that every proverb has its opposite. For every *Time is money* there is a *Stop and smell the roses.*  When someone says *You never stand in the same river twice* someone else has already replied *There is nothing new under the sun.*  In the mind's arithmetic, 1 plus −1 equals 2. Truths are not quantities but scripts: Become for a moment the mind in which this is true.

27.
The viruses that co-opt the machinery of our cells;  the stories we allow to enter and explain us.

28.
If the wise knew everything the foolish know, there would be no fools.

29.
Pain is not a democracy.

30.

Often my child asks for something utterly trivial not because she cares for it but because she needs to hear me say *Yes, yes.*

31.

Never treat the sadness of a friend as an accusation, though it is.

32.

If you're Larkin or Bishop, one book a decade is enough. If you're not? More than enough.

33.

No gift is ever exactly right for me. But why do I suppose the gift is for me, or my gratitude for the giver?

34.

Where I touch you lightly enough, there I am also touched.

35.

It's easy to renounce the world till you see who picks up what you renounced.

36.

I say I have left gods behind.  But who is that Luck who will one day mail me my rescue? Who is the Grudger for whose sake I knock on wood and delay counting my chickens? On Whose account do I usher bad thoughts quickly out of my head lest they be overheard? Who are the Ghosts whose watching is the heat between my shoulder blades?  Given that most of my day is helpless credulity, creeds are superfluous, skepticism affected.

37.

As much innocence is found as lost.

38.

The world is not what anyone wished for, but it's what everyone wished for.

39.

The will is weak. Good thing, or we'd succeed in governing our lives with our stupid ideas!

40.

Wind cannot blow the wind away, nor water wash away the water.

41.

If you do everything for one reason, then all you have done will become meaningless when the reason does.

42.

Decades later, I dream long dreams of my brother alive. Or I am still in my first marriage, and childless: none of what I now call my life has been thought of. Does this mean that news travels slowly, that there are still great strata of the brain waiting to feel shocks we thought had reached our cores? More likely, the stories we tell ourselves of the past and the present, the possible and the fantastic, exist in the mind separately from the secondary characteristics *no longer* or *not real*. How lightly, closing my eyes, that connection between the image and its status is deranged. I realize more and more that some idea or love or scene I have only thought of all these years has become as important as what actually happened, realer.

43.

Do we return again and again to our losses to get back what we had or lose what remains?

44.

Once it's gone, how easy to say it was mine.

45.

I have to start over and over on the loves and books that most possess me, so fine the difference is between knowing and not knowing them.

46.

We invent a great Loss to convince ourselves we have a beginning. But loss is a current: the coolness of one side of a wet finger held up, the faint hiss in your ears at midnight, water sliding over the dam at the back of your mind, memory unremembering itself.

47.

Looking back: youth, innocence, energy, desire. But none of it's as amazing as all we were sure we *had to do*.

48.

Suppose you had to remember to beat your heart, contract in exact sequence the muscles you use for every step, and run your mitochondria and ion channels. Conservatism comes out of the body, the sense of many things being done for us that any attempt to re-think, or even make conscious, would fatally disrupt.

49.

No matter who you love, you make love to a woman and a man.

50.

Not beauty, not even need. We fall in love because we are unused—the less used, the more foolishly we fall.

51.

Of all our self-delusions, none is more exhausting or transparent than that of our indispensability. But it keeps telling us we are generous to remain deceived.

52.

Value yourself according to the burdens you carry, and you will find everything a burden.

53.

Lake: earth's idea of sky.

54.

Patience is not very different from courage. It just takes longer.

55.

Easier to keep changing your life than to live it.

56.

In clearing out files, ideas, hopes, throw away a little too much. Pruning only dead wood will not encourage growth.

57.

It's not that reason kills faith; reason is the lesser faith that steers us when we have already lost a greater one.

58.

*Like.* Late afternoon, a pale cirrus crosses the nearly transparent moon. They are so alike, meeting, that I feel, suddenly and childishly, *They* like *each other.* Somehow I can't help liking them for that. Somehow I can't help feeling that they like me liking them.

59.

When she was little her face rose up before me, reading, driving. Even now I cannot have her out of my sight for thirty seconds in a supermarket. But she will leave home, and there will be whole days I hardly think of her. Between this beginning and that ending is a story I cannot admit I am being told. Compared to it, what is the failure of my work, our language, the planet?

60.

The saints and the sinners say the same thing about life: *Only for a moment.*

61.

Even to say *I believe nothing* how much you have to believe.

62.

Of course we're enraged when Authority bores us: that right we give only to our intimates.

63.

I have to deserve my joys. So do my enemies. For those I love, my standards are more sensible.

64.

God help my neighbors if I loved them as I love myself.

65.

A dog will mistake your singing for a call to follow.

66.

I surely don't understand most things as well as I think I do, since I don't understand why people bother to say them.

67.

Pity the man who knows everything, for he has to fear surprise.

68.

The poem in the quarterly is sure to fail within two lines: flaccid, rhythmless, hopelessly dutiful. But I read poets from strange languages with freedom and pleasure because I can believe in all that has been lost in translation. Though all works, all acts, all languages are already translation.

69.

The tyrant has first imagined he is a victim.

70.

Weakness keeps the gate.

71.

We do not love money. But once we have it, it is not *money*—it is *ours*.

72.

Millions of perfect crimes are committed every day, by no one.

73.

When I returned to the scene there were, as I expected, the police lines and photojournalists, but there were so many others hoping to be accused.

74.

You can't pretend you're just watching the actors. Someone a little further away will see you acting the part of a watcher.

75.

On what is valuable thieves and the law agree.

76.

If men could steal happiness, they would not have to steal anything else.

77.

The tyrant puts down his own rebellion, everywhere.

78.

What clings to good moments, or labors to repeat them?  Not happiness, which is what lets you let them go.

79.

Desire, make me poor again.

80.

Success repeats itself until it is failure.

81.

The worst helplessness is forgetting there is help.

82.

If it can be used again, it is not wisdom but theory.

83.

Evil will rule you; goodness will not, though you are good.

84.

In the long run, the single sin is less of a problem than the good reasons for it.

85.
The great consolation of righteousness is never having to worry whether you're a bore.

86.
Compared to typing it is still half in the mind, still simultaneous like thought: my illegible script. *Beast* and *heart* are the same, *ravish* and *vanish, younger* and *enough*.

87.
Every rule is an exception to another rule.

88.
Each question asks, too, why it had to be asked.

89.
For each thing we do to change, we do a million to remain the same.

90.
The new day is still a day.

91.
What I'm not changes more than what I am.

92.

All but the most durable books serve us simply by opening a window on all we wanted to say and feel and think about. We may not even notice that they have not said it themselves till we go back to them years later and do not find what we loved in them. You cannot keep the view by taking the window with you.

93.

Wind, ocean, fire: the things we like to liken our passions to don't break, can't stop.

94.

My weaknesses are less remarkable than all the things I have at one time or another imagined were my strengths.

95.

You do not have to be a fire to keep one burning.

96.

Despair says *It's all the same.* Happiness can distinguish a thousand Despairs.

97.
*But for this rock*, its shadow says, *I could get at the sun.*

98.
The ruts are deepest in the middle of the road.

99.
We wouldn't take so many chances if we really believed in chance.

100.
A belief is a question we have put aside so we can get on with what we believe we have to do.

101.
The safest thing to talk about is change.

102.
If you keep your mouth shut, no one can swing you around by the tongue.

103.

The mind does not understand the heart? Neither does the heart.

104.

Stand watch over your peace and you will be peaceless.

105.

So many times I've made myself stupid with the fear of being outsmarted.

106.

The wound hurts less than your desire to wound me.

107.

Those who are too slow to be intelligent deserve our patience, those who are too quick, our pity.

108.

Think of all the smart people made stupid by flaws of character. The finest watch isn't fine long when used as a hammer.

109.

If you reason far enough you will come to unreasonable conclusions.

110.

Who has no mercy on himself will have none on you.

111.

Language cannot be exact enough to prove anything absolutely or rule anything out. Past a certain point, more precision in argument becomes less, not more, scientific, like measuring the diameter of a proton to six significant figures with a yardstick. Thinkers, whatever they pretend, count on our mercy. Perfect rigor proves nothing but distrust.

112.

The first abuse of power is not realizing that you have it.

113.

Education is so slow, disorganized, accidental that sometimes it seems I could have relaxed for forty years and then learned everything I know in a few months of really efficient study. Then again, I'm not sure what I know.

114.

Greater than the temptations of beauty are those of method.

115.

Of very few subjects can it be said that the order in which we would teach them is the order in which we really learned them. The beginning is what we first see when we get to the end and turn around.

116.

If I didn't spend so much time writing, I'd know a lot more. But I wouldn't know anything.

117.

Singing is a way of remembering to breathe.

118.

Everyone has the same secrets. That is the secret we keep best.

119.

You will know the real god by your fear of loving it.

120.

Only the dead have discovered what they cannot live without.

121.

The worst part of fear is not knowing what to do. And often you only have to ask *What would I do if I were not afraid?* to know what to do, and do it, and not be afraid.

122.

To think yourself incapable of crime is one failure of imagination. To think yourself capable of all crimes is another.

123.

Theories of happiness are somehow less troubled by the misfortunes of the deserving than by all those people who are happy and couldn't possibly be.

124.

There are crimes I don't commit mainly because I don't want to find out I could.

125.

The questioner is my jailer. His questions are not his, though my answers would be mine.

126.

The passions, it has been said, are the only orators that convince, meaning they overcome reason. No, the passions are what reasoning was invented for. The drives were nature's first provision: thinking was added later, to get us around the world's obstacles to them. When we find ourselves arguing internally, the obstacle is not reason but some other passion.

127.

To me the great divide is between the talkative and the quiet. Do they just say everything that's on their minds, even *before* it's on their minds? Sometimes I think I could just turn up my head like a Walkman so what's going on there could be heard by others. But there would still be a difference. For inside the head they are talking to people like them, and I am talking to someone like me: he is quiet and doesn't much like being talked at; he can't conceal how easily he gets bored.

128.

Intimates: the ones it's hardest to tell everything you're thinking.

129.

Most creatures find what they need by descending unthinkingly the slope of chemical concentrations, best thought of as odors. To few is given the ability to see with any clarity where they are going. Thought is the imaginative extension of the eyes. Or is it the legs?

130.

Actions speak louder than words. But how I say is what I do.

131.

Harder to laugh at the comedy if it's about you, harder to cry at the tragedy if it isn't.

132.

Easier to cry at a silly movie than for your own sadness, easier to laugh at another than at yourself. If you manage that harder laughter, it is because you see what others see. And if you cry for yourself, unless with the most powerful grief, it is because you have cast yourself in a role so melodramatic you can weep as one of the watchers.

133.

Even at the movies, we laugh together, we weep alone.

134.

If the saints are perfect and unwavering we are excused from trying to imitate them. Also if they are not.

135.

Success is whatever humiliation everyone has agreed to compete for.

136.

Loving your enemies takes away their right to hate you. Kinder to endure being the enemy they need.

137.

Tragic hero, madman, addict, fatal lover. We exalt those who cannot escape their fates because we cannot stay inside our own.

138.

No one desired is unchanged: the god of many cannot remain the true god.

139.

There is a moment falling asleep when you can't tell whether voices are in the room or in your head. Wide awake, you may be embarrassed or cross if your imaginary conversation with someone is interrupted by the person himself, as if he might have heard. Our thinking about our lives is dramatic: scenes and scripts and voices. I'm surprised that multiple personalities are so much less common in reality than in fiction: what a little disorder it would take, a distraction, a sleep, for one of our minor characters to imagine *he* was the star, to speak out for everyone else. And that's what it would be, a change of billing, not of authorship. For you do not write your play—you are just the character in it called *The Playwright*. The real writer, you never meet.

140.

Naturalness is whatever part we are most comfortable acting.

141.

There might have been a god before Creation, but by now he must be bewildered in all our suffering and fantasy, like a man in a dream he cannot remember to wake up from.

142.

Growth is barely controlled damage.

143.

I drowse, wake with a start, having dreamt of tripping, or falling from a window, or trying to brake a car a pedestrian has just stepped in front of. This is the mind's fear of letting the body go, as it must, lest we act out our dreams. Then there is the dream, just before waking, of calling the body back. You try to run, weak-kneed. You want to call out but can hardly find your voice. And in between these partings and reunions, like lovers, mind and body dream of what they might do together.

144.

Why would they need Realism if they were sure they were real?

145.

In these times, the tragic passions do not end in death. They split me, and we live on.

146.

Seizing on a piece of business, I become tiny, eager, efficient: roiled water I cannot see into. But to really live is to expand like a pupil in the dark, like a pool gradually seen into. If I do not waste time, I am wasting my time.

147.

The procrastinator dreads beginning, the workaholic, ending. Each inhabits a parenthesis fending off Time. Every lit cigarette is a bridge over Time's emptiness, each quest or project or hope. Even dread of death is just another way to make Time a story we can bear to listen to.

148.

Imagination is the only true waste: the rest is producing and consuming. And much of what passes for imagination is only obsession, which is just another kind of productivity, giving you what you want again and again and again.

149.

Money and love both say they are all you need.

150.

They say productivity is the key to confidence, and confidence... to productivity. And they're happy walking back and forth between these two rooms, each the excuse for the other.

151.

I sell my time to get enough money to buy it back.

152.

Addiction, profession, virtue. Anything is a game if its rules are simpler than time's.

153.

To lose weight or regain patience, learn to love the sour, the bitter, the salty, the clear.

154.

Only eternity needs eternity. But without the year, no growth; without the hour, no love; without the second, no grace, no thought.

155.

What did you do today? *Nothing* say our little children, and so do I. What we most are is what we keep mistaking for nothing. Everything we notice is just news.

156.

We search for things we cannot resist as if desperate to prove we still have passions. Addiction is our metaphor. I give it up.

157.

*I'll buy that* means also *I believe it.* Your choices: spend, and believe in things; save, and believe in money.

158.

Whoever loves his disease must be cured of love to be cured.

159.

Passions are the great defense against passion.

160.

When I want to change myself, I invent a new rule, like a revolutionist who has discovered he believes neither in freedom nor in those he intended to free.

161.

Priceless things cannot be bought, though they are often sold.

162.

Everyone loves the Revolution. We only disagree on whether it has occurred.

163.

A day is only a day. But a life is only a life.

164.

The hard of hearing cannot tell their voices are loud.

165.

I don't know what's meant by *Know thyself,* which seems to ask a window to look at a window. I aspire to know when best to walk or eat, which music I need, and how to keep myself sitting as I am now, stubbornly enraptured with doing practically nothing. These are like the things people learn who have to start persnickety cars in the cold, or get the most out of exhausted fields.

166.

Beware of knowing your virtues; you may lose them. Beware of knowing your vices; you may forgive them.

167.

I say I have no self-knowledge, but I know which things I will never tell you.

168.

No price fluctuates so wildly as that of time.

169.

*He is sincere,* we say, meaning there is nothing else to be said.

170.

To be sincere is one thing. To practice Sincerity is to burden everyone else with believing you.

171.

To know, you just have to know. To believe, you have to make others believe.

172.

No one is saved by love or reason.

173.

Shop: for shoes in the afternoon, when the foot is largest; for groceries overfed, when nothing pleases.

174.

Debts of a certain immensity demand betrayal.

175.

Do not blame the fire for knowing one thing.

176.

When it rains you discover which things you did not want out in the rain.

177.

Ah, *other* people. How definite and decisive they are, whether hateful or admirable. Stretched in lawn chairs when the wind comes, they shall lift into Heaven, driven by laws too simple to believe in.

178.

If you say *All is well*, I believe you. If I say *All is well*, I'm abbreviating.

179.

Every life is allocated one hundred seconds of true genius. They might be enough. If we could just be sure which ones they were.

180.

Can the wind-carved stone know the wind is gone?

181.

*It is clear,* we say, as if to see through something were to know it.

182.

The wind says everything except *The wind has died.*

183.

I know which disasters could be mine by how dangerous pity is.

184.

I scorn those who believe more, and envy them, pity those who believe less, and fear them.

185.

The guy who slathers the Congressman with red paint? The zealot, the terrorist? Under my disdain, a strange gratitude for those I disagree with. They keep me from having to take too seriously the moments when I disagree with myself. I need them to be the people I don't want to be.

186.

Absence makes the heart grow fonder: then it is only distance that separates us.

187.

If you want to know how they could forget you, wait till you forget them.

188.

Experience is being a little surer of what won't ever happen.

189.

My natural self was so defective that it was long ago retired in favor of this remodeled one, instincts monitored and re-directed, reflexes interrupted and subject to review. But I do not know who could have done this.

190.

We are never so aware of how we look to others as when we have a great secret. Vanity always thinks it has a great secret.

191.

*Throw it away.* But there is no *away.*

192.

Every December the real cold may never come.
Every March it may never go away.

193.

Happiness is a sad study.

194.

No matter how fast you travel, life walks.

195.

The best way to know your faults is to notice
which ones you accuse others of.

196.

To condemn your sin in another is hypocrisy.
Not to condemn is to reserve your right to
sin.

197.

Let me have my dreams but not what I dream
of.

198.

Out of a decade we remember the few minutes
we have not been able to make into ourselves.

199.

Every time you say *In two weeks...* they are sub-
tracted from your life.

200.

When your eyes widen in the dark, what is
trying to get out?

201.

A little spill holds all the depth of the sky.

202.

Love needs something to forgive as much as
something to love.

203.

The future is pure luck. But once it arrives
it begins to seem explainable. Not long after-
wards, it could hardly have happened other-
wise.

204.

By looking for the origins of things we deceive
ourselves about their inevitability. Things that
did not happen also have origins.

205.

Who would be slave to his passions if they did not also feel like freedom?

206.

What we talked ourselves out of was a whim. What we did *anyway* was a passion. So it seems now. But later, how confusing the difference between passion and predictability. And the thing we felt free to dismiss comes to seem our freedom.

207.

Sometimes I hate beauty because I don't have any choice about loving it. I must be wrong in this, but whether because I take freedom too seriously, or love, I cannot tell.

208.

If you change your mind, you are free. Or you were.

209.
Nature is not that prejudiced against the past. Yesterday is only a little less likely to happen next than any one of the zillion possible tomorrows that does.

210.
If there is a calm after youth, it comes not from feeling less but from being able, sometimes, to decide when to feel, where in the mind to be.

211.
When you sense from some almost-blush of the brain that you are about to remember something embarrassing, but push it down before you can see what it is. When you wake in the small hours and un-think a thought that would have kept you up. When you stand in front of a crowd and slide a hand along a dark wall in your mind to find the switch that will turn off your fear, or the other switch that will make you excited enough to excite them. Where are these lids and erasers and switches, how do we learn to find them, why can't they always be found?

212.
Happiness is not the only happiness.

213.
The best friends are those who have already forgiven you your worst.

214.
Someone's deceleration to exit, read a sign or rubberneck starts a little chain of responses that becomes a five-mile backup. So much of what turns out to be the huge evil of systems is the amplification of tiny reluctances to let go of a habit, to lift a phone, to look up and meet someone's eyes.

215.
A tornado can't stack two dimes.

216.
The mistakes I made from weakness embarrass me far less than those I made insisting on my strength.

217.
All the falling rain is caught.

218.

The silly, incompetent dead, so much they forgot to tell us about how to live! All we can learn from their books is that others have found their own way and we may yet.

219.

It takes more than one life to be sure what's killing you.

220.

Later you will not want it. Does that mean you should take it now or let it go?

221.

More than you remember stays green all winter.

222.

Worry wishes life were over.

223.

The ambitious: those who have to work longer to find a place where it seems safe to stop.

224.

Water deepens where it has to wait.

225.

Minds go from intuition to articulation to self-defense, which is what they die of.

226.

Nothing is more real than what's impossible.

227.

I am saving good deeds to buy a great sin.

228.

Governments, banks and loves collapse when all decide simultaneously to take all that is owed them.

229.

The shortest distance between two points is deciding they are the same.

230.

Some things, like faith, cheer, courage, you can give when you do not have them.

231.
Surviving another argument we find that what kept us apart was fear of separation.

232.
More can be learned than taught.

233.
If I belch at the table I am embarrassed. But not so much if no one hears. Or if you pretend not to have heard. Or I pretend I do not know you heard. Or you pretend you do not know I know.

234.
Why should the whole lake have the same name?

235.
My troubles are tedious even to me, and require no sympathy. I told them only so I wouldn't be wanting to tell them.

236.

It seems I am always managing difficult people.
But maybe what seems their difficulty is their
managing of me.

237.

How much less difficult life is when you do
not want anything from people. And yet you
owe it to them to want something.

238.

Music is the highest art, no question. But lit-
erature is a friendlier one. It depends on us
more, bores us more quickly, can't go on if we
don't, can't stop saying what it means, can't
stop giving us something to forgive.

239.

You had better study the degrees of yielding
lest you have only two choices: to be hard, to
be someone else.

240.

Self-love is not one of the passions; it is forget-
ting there is anything to be passionate about.

241.

Self-love, strange name. Since it feels neither like loving someone, nor like being loved.

242.

If I can keep giving you what you want, I may not have to love you.

243.

I believe in nothing. But I'd prefer that you did not agree with me.

244.

If I satisfied all my needs, I would still need them.

245.

Who gives his heart away too easily must have a heart under his heart.

246.

I know what I look best in, but looking your best is only one idea of how to dress. Sometimes I want to look like a tree. Or indifference. Or you.

247.

It's amazing that I sit at my job all day and no one sees me clearly enough to say *What is that boy doing behind a desk?*

248.

Who breaks the thread, the one who pulls, the one who holds on?

249.

Writing is like washing windows in the sun. With every attempt to perfect clarity you make a new smear.

250.

The wounds you do not want to heal are you.

251.

Impatience is not wanting to understand that you don't understand.

252.

It's so much easier to get further from home than nearer that all men become travelers.

253.
Back then I wanted to be right about my estimate of my abilities. Now I want to be wrong.

254.
Idolaters of the great need to believe that what they love cannot fail them; adorers of camp, kitsch, trash that they cannot fail what they love.

255.
No criticism so sharp as seeing they think you need to be flattered.

256.
Time heals.  By taking even more.

257.
The one who hates you perfectly loves you.

258.
The spirals around the galactic core, the coin of hair over the drain, the mind looking down into itself—each formed by a hole it just barely avoids falling into.

259.

The most common addiction is to anxiety.

260.

I stopped reading stories when I was no longer able to confuse love with justice.

261.

Turn on the light and you will see, but it will not be darkness that you see.

262.

Competition and sympathy are joined at the root, as may be seen in the game *My grief is greater than yours*, which no one can keep himself from playing.

263.

How fix the unhappy couple, when it was happiness they loved in each other?

264.

After a while of losing you, I become the one who has lost you. Did the pain change me, or did I change to lessen the pain?

265.
Experience tends to immunize against experience, which is why the most experienced are not the wisest.

266
The mind that's too sensitive feels mostly itself.
A little hardness makes us softer for others.

267.
Fewer regret wasting a year than never having wasted one.

268.
To be admired costs less than to be loved.

269.
What is most remarkable about dreams is not their bizarreness but how rarely we experience them as bizarre. They must contribute silently to our faith that we could live through anything.

270.
Praise thinks it knows you.

271.

While I am laughing at you, asshole, I do not hate you very much. But I am not doing *you* any favors. My hate, after all, happens to *me*.

272.

Skunk cabbage, bitter dandelion, onion grass, asparagus that makes your urine reek. Things that come up early in the spring had better disgust lest they be eaten straight off. I wonder if their economies are like ours, if their bad taste arises from the very antifreeze that allows them to endure harsh weather.

273.

You who have proved how much like me you are: how could I trust you?

274.

A secret is the illusion that confessing it would make a difference.

275.

A shower of magnolia, a gust of lilac and suddenly I am a well something huge is falling down, as if I were in love. Why did evolution do this? Surely dizzy boys burying their faces in hyacinths were never significant pollinators? Yet somehow these plants know us better than we know ourselves (was it the tree, rather than Daphne, that Apollo wanted?). Maybe the lesson is the incongruity of desire: you shall find in love no way out, into what you love no entrance, and must be glad to feel you will die for it.

276.

No garden without weeds? No weeds without gardens.

277.

Memory's not infinite. If I looked at this pitted and pocked wall microscopically enough the visual data would fill my brain entirely. Against this, boredom and reflex generalization protect me. If I call up the wall in memory, some generic version will be made up—I never see *nothing,* I never see gaps or error messages where I have forgotten or mistaken. Same even with those cherished early memories: we call up a sketch, fill in the blanks, and store it again, changed. There is no virgin past. The mind is like one of those floating islands of vegetation whose roots grasp not the earth but each other.

278.

There are only three subjects—death, love and justice. All of them are depicted as blind.

279.

God needs us to believe in him so he can believe in nothing.

280.
When you walk from a dark house into noon, you know it is brighter, but you do not feel it as a hundred times brighter, which it may well be, or a thousand times louder. The death of a thousand is not a thousand times more painful than the death of one. The mind is buffered, lest the ordinary minutes tear us apart, and perhaps in this is the root of all generalization and abstraction. The extremes of joy and sorrow are easily reached, even in the same hour. What we call "perfect happiness" and "perfect misery" have less to do with intensity than with duration and reliability. They are matters of hope.

281.
Envy, bitterness, disdain: failure to be alone.

282.
The blind, who read our faces with their hands, must feel we are always ready to be struck or touched.

283.

While I stand on line, my face goes slack as I daydream. When it's my turn, the teller looks at me, frightened. What has he seen there?

284.

Believe stupid praise, deserve stupid criticism.

285.

I need a much larger vocabulary to talk to you than to talk to myself.

286.

Why can we read character in a face? Partly because the child with that face was treated as the character that seemed to belong to it, and so acted it and grew into it. One comfort of middle age is seeing around us the dozens who have finally grown beyond what their faces and indeed their bodies said they were.

287.

Of course you could ruin me, but then I would know you.

288.

Determinism. How romantic to think the mind a machine reliable enough to transform the same causes over and over again into the same effects. When even toasters fail!

289.

No use placing mystical trust in the body. It is perfectly adapted to life a million years ago— eat while you can, flee, strike—but what does it know about cities, love, speculation? Nor will evolution change it, since failure now leads not to death and subtraction from the gene pool but merely to misery.

290.

Even your great deeds are not all yours. There are days you are someone who couldn't have done them, or someone who wishes you hadn't.

291.

If I didn't have so much work to keep me from it, how would I know what I wanted to do?

292.

It gets harder and harder to be free. Every time I need a larger labor to be at the end of.

293.

He may not deserve your praise, but he deserves to be treated as if some day he might.

294.

Wind shakes the flame but feeds the fire.

295.

The best way to get people to do what you want is not to be too particular about what you want them to do.

296.

Do not wait for a clear desk or a windless day.

297.

While everyone clamored at the god, I kept aloof, scorning their selfishness. Now that he has ascended, I hate him because he does not guess what I want.

298.
Red photons have the lowest energy, blue the highest.  Which color then for blood, water? Body, sky?  Passion, distance?

299.
That gentle, harmless drug that would make me permanently happier?  I would refuse it. After all, I can't tell myself from my limits.  It would be like dying for a great cause: nothing of me would be left to know what I'd done. And I am no hero.

300.
I forget the future, but when it happens I remember.

301.
My good deeds need as much forgiveness as my sins.

302.
The lies I was ready to tell also count against me.

303.

A truth is said over and over until it's heard once, then unheard because it is too true.

304.

Go outside?   At least here I know what I am inside.

305.

When we are not waiting for anything, poor creatures, we wait for something to wait for.

306.

When you laughed at me, I could have been free, but instead of laughing with you, I clung to my imprisonment.

307.

Do not ask the roads whether it is good to travel.

308.

Nothing happens so faithfully as Never.

309.

What we have is given again and again. It must be so, since not to have is to be continually denied.

310.

Each of the tastes, each of the colors is a marvel. All of them together are nothing.

311.

A man with one idea has none.

312.

I could explain, but then you would understand my explanation, not what I said.

313.

Pleased is pleasing.

314.

First he gathered what he needed. Then he needed to keep gathering what he used to need.

315.

I speak so you will speak, extend my hand so
you will extend yours, ask how you're doing,
whether you love me. I do these experiments
over and over since, while I was looking the
other way, the laws of the universe might well
have altered.

316.

The road forgets what's underneath the road.

317.

When I slipped on the ice, I laughed, as if I
myself were some joke I had fallen for.

318.

The obvious was not necessarily obvious be-
fore you heard it.

319.

There would be no god if we could keep our-
selves from praying.

320.

Everything but pain is a hobby.

321.

What attracts me to some people is the part that does not know I am there; but then it does.

322.

How strong my weakness is!

323.

I keep glimpsing the loneliness I want, my thoughts without me.

324.

The bold do not fool me. They are not bold enough to wait.

325.

The best disguise is the one everyone else is wearing.

326.

*Once bitten, twice shy,* it is said. Yet we make the same mistakes over and over. Nature knows it is less important to escape pain than to avoid exceptionless rules.

327.

Believe everything a little. The credulous know things the skeptical do not.

328.

The knife disappears with sharpening.

329.

Envy, pretense, shame are among the diseases that can be cured either by more modesty or more pride. No wonder. With the merest touch of resentment or insistence, modesty becomes pride. And pride that is unself-conscious, claiming nothing, we call modesty.

330.

Some things are too difficult to succeed at, some too easy.

331.

He always wants to know what *the best* is so he can be superior to everything at once by seeing that the best isn't perfect.

332.

It is not themselves that the proud love. They are, at every moment, like someone who has just decided to buy something.

333.

Life speaks so slowly that I cannot hear, but I wake one morning and understand something it seems no one has told me.

334.

If you're tempted to think words powerless, think how much harm yours have done by accident.

335.

No matter how much time I save, I have only now.

336.

Pleasure is for you. Joy is for itself.

337.

The dead are still writing. Every morning, somewhere, is a line, a passage, a whole book you are sure wasn't there yesterday.

338.

The happy and the suffering probably under-
stand life equally well, but the sufferers may
see a little more clearly how little it is that they
understand.

339.

Everywhere he looked Nerval saw a black spot.
That one's easy, but where the optic nerve
enters the retina there is another one, quite
literally a blind spot. We never notice: the
brain, like a mother softening the bad news,
continually fills it in, never letting us know
there is nothing there. O, spot I never see,
from you I learn my landscapes are movies,
my words a greeting card, my memories an
official explanation!

340.

What you fear to believe, your children will
believe.

341.

There are silences harder to take back than
words.

342.

Of our first few years we remember nothing: experience only slowly gives us the power to be formed by experience. If this were not true, our characters would be completely determined by our infant hours of confusion, pain and helplessness, and we would all be the same. For her first six months my daughter cried continuously, who knows why. Yet she is as happy and trusting and kind as if all that had never happened. It never did.

343.

A man having trouble with a hammer talks it onto the nail. A lot of what seems like talking to others is steering oneself. And a lot of talking to oneself is like hammering another.

344.

To paranoids and the Elect everything makes sense.

345.

Art is long, they say, life short. Art ends, though, and life doesn't.

346.

At first life is too slow, so we take to books. In the novel children grow up in a sentence and a young man wakes up gray and over. Also in life. And then we open books to slow down what we missed.

347.

I am delighted to discover my weaknesses. ("Discover," I repeat, rather than "exhibit" or "be criticized for"). As if I had just met a new citizen of myself, and was glad to find his good points. Am I timid and indecisive? Then I am flexible and tolerant of ambiguity. Am I crippled by self-consciousness? At least I see what I'm doing. I will gladly try on any shape, as long as I can decide myself to take it off.

348.

The New gets old much faster than the Old gets older.

349.

The man who sticks to his plan will become what he used to want to be.

350.
No debt burdens like the fear of debt.

351.
Those who pride themselves on always telling the truth generally concentrate on truths more painful to others than to themselves.

352.
Laziness is the sin most willingly confessed to, since it implies talents greater than have yet appeared.

353.
If we were really sure we were one of a kind, there would be no envy. My envy demeans both of us—no wonder it is the hardest sin to confess. It says I am not who I think I am unless I have what you have. It says that you are what you have, and I could have it.

354.
A man's rage at love is a rage to be more deeply deceived.

355.

Envy is ashamed of itself. If it weren't hanging back, it would go all the way to emulation and love.

356.

You would think we would envy only what we love, for being loveable. But no, we envy those the world loves, because we care less for being worthy of love than being loved.

357.

Big decisions threaten to narrow us, as if we would no longer be, after choosing, the person who could have chosen otherwise. Looking into the future, we see ourselves completely defined by one choice—to be someone's lover, to take such and such a job. We become flat characters in a novel, and die a little.

358.

I have so much trouble choosing that I wish restaurants would ask me for a list of things I absolutely will not eat, and then select a dish at random from the rest. In that case, I would only have to figure out how it was good in itself, and not why I again failed to know what would make me happiest.

359.

The road not taken is the part of you not taking the road.

360.

When my friend does something stupid, he is just my friend doing something stupid. When I do something stupid, I have deeply betrayed myself.

361.

A god, choosing, becomes human.

362.

Embarrassment and guilt console us. They imply we have a purer self that we have somehow betrayed. Regret, too, is a disguise of hope, convincing us that things could have gone better, and therefore that they may.

363.

My deepest regrets, if I am honest, are not things I wish were otherwise, but things I wish I wish were otherwise.

364.

The head learns quickly and forgets. The heart learns slowly and, since it cannot forget, must betray itself to move on.

365.

Your hatred is a night bombardment, lighting places of myself I never see. But even in the pain of admitting my selfishness there is curiosity and relief. To be a character, at last, and a rather ordinary one, from whom I realistically needn't expect too much!

366.

During the hottest months, the sun is moving away from us, during the coldest, coming back.

367.

We lose the tendency in the fact, forgetting that the days lengthen all winter, shorten all summer. The painter, adding a hairline of sky, to a red, red canvas enters his blue period. We lose the fact in the tendency, forgetting that every act and utterance are against a wind. A man recommending quiet is not wishing immediately to be a stone. A man wishing to be a stone is in less danger from his wish than from what he wished it against.

368.

A fern is the spreading of its fronds, but also what keeps it from being an ocean of green.

369.

Why shouldn't you read this the way I wrote it, with days between the lines?

370.

What we love and fear in passion is dispropor-
tion. It is too large to have been caused, to be
satisfied, to be ours.

371.

What but things highly metaphorical could
Gulliver have done with his six-inch woman?
Yet desire is always a disproportion, a meta-
phor. It's a curious and naive error to insist
triumphantly that everything stands for sex
when sex does not even stand for itself.

372.

Called into question, I drive away embar-
rassment with anger. Caught up in anger, I
find that regret or self-doubt will defuse it.
Bereft or rejected, I waver between sadness
and resentment. To choose the harder feeling
is to see the division as between us, to choose
the softer is to acknowledge it within me. Yet
anger says *There is so much of you that remains*
and sadness *It was myself that might have been
lost.*

373.
Embarrassment is the greatest teacher, but since its lessons are exactly those we have tried hardest to conceal from ourselves, it may teach us, also, to perfect our self-deception.

374.
I trick myself into sins I could not forgive myself for intending. If I could depend on myself for a little mercy, I would perhaps not have grown so expert in the self-deception that makes it so difficult minute to minute to know what I am really doing.

375.

We call desire infinite when it seems larger
than the things we ask it to do, which is the
usual case. Sometimes I call up a great wind
of it to blow the smoke out of the soul, chill a
line, nudge a word a little out of its socket. Yet
it may be stronger when it stays in one place,
sending down roots, making talk, pushing a
weight too slowly to be seen, and subtler when
it is drawing us into a pear, a paving stone, the
blue of tree shade. Then we are not tempted
to call it infinite. When it fits like that, we are
not even tempted to call it desire.

376.

You keep track of your worth on some wildly
cyclic stock market that will soar in fantasy,
crash at a cold glance. Other people think you
never change.

377.

If only we were satisfied to have others think
of us what we think of them.

378.

Walking home one winter sunset, "visionary dreariness:" fine as hairs, the intricacy of black trees against the weakly yellow, chill horizon. So strange I think it isn't real—someone should turn on the lights, let me see what's really there. So beautiful and moving in its very bleakness that I think, as I often do, *Words couldn't convey this. No one will ever know about this but me.* I forget that this is mostly my mood—a camera wouldn't get it either. And yet the *can't say* of beauty, more than its transience, is the melancholy that Keats knows is in "the very temple of delight." The nightingale sings and the "heart aches" because it is moved. Moved where? Moved *to.* To translate, or to translate itself—to know or become what it has just heard—but none of our media are equivalent. Not sight and sound, or dreaming and waking, or language and anything. And you could think *But thousands of people are watching this sunset,* or you could think *Why does the exact image matter?* Everyone knows what these moods are. But then you would not have been in a mood to be hurt by a sky or the song of a bird.

379.

I never go to the mirror unless there's something I am hoping not to see.

380.

What *objects* of desire? O but the *in,* and the *to,* ah the *of!*

381.

What exhausts imagination is fear of exhausting it. The gods detest hoarders, giving nothing to those who do not trust them to give.

382.

Travel light: necessity invents.

383.

A screwdriver is for screws. When you pry open a paint can with it, you have committed metaphor, which is the second use of things, their will gone. As for us, since we don't know what our purpose is, all we do is metaphorical.

384.

A faith is dead when no one can think of a heresy.

385.

Nothing so hampers creativity as having all the right tools.

386.

A child's toys teach her how to talk to herself. We are our own toys.

387.

Why would we worry what others think of us if their opinions did not change us?

388.

Each planet has its distance, and each friend.

389.

The more reasons you give for refusing, the more it will seem you have no reason but unwillingness.

390.

The best time is stolen time.

391.

What we usually call laziness is undeclared anxiety. Real laziness comes from the angels.

392.

Succeed and the world becomes just.

393.

Get fat and you will call hunger one of the virtues.

394.

As hard as other people are to talk to, I'm glad I don't have to sit next to myself.

395.

Disillusionment is also an illusion.

396.

That I have thought all the evil thoughts does not mean they are mine.

397.
The mind notices it exists when it gets in its own way, as two strands have to get in each others' way to make a knot. What's important in *I think, therefore I am* is less the statement than the stumble.

398.
Any virtue systematically applied becomes a vice. Morality is attention, not system.

399.
Say nothing as if it were news.

400.
I lie so I do not have to trust you to believe.

401.
The greatest lie I was ever told tried, O tried, to be true.

402.

We hasten to condemn the deceiver in love, yet the deceived falls in everyone's estimate, not least his own. He has been sold below cost by the one it seems should know his value best.

403.

I lied. And my embarrassment was so great that I changed everything else to make the lie true.

404.

I lust for more strangeness because I have turned everything too easily into myself.

405.

Say too soon what you think and you will say what everyone else thinks.

406.

If god had been more easily bored, we would look less like each other, more like oceans, contraptions, birds, gods.

407.
When I re-married, I started remembering things—the smell of yarrow, words of my father—I hadn't thought of in years, as if they had suddenly become necessary to the new self that was organizing. The mind is like a well-endowed museum, only a small fraction of its holdings on view at any one time, and this is true from hour to hour as well as from era to era. I am different tones, capacities, intelligences, memories when I am phoning on business, walking by the canal, or waiting with that finely tensed blankness for a line to write itself. For the most part, there is nothing romantic about the unconscious. It starts as the sentence we did not say, the love we did not use. It is as substantial or insubstantial as the shadow of a house, in which some things will grow, some not. Which moves as the sun moves.

408.
Pebble, question, soul: no one can see all sides at once, but there is no side that cannot be seen.

409.

I am hugely overpaid.  Except compared to the people I work with.

410.

There is no future till you underestimate the past.

411.

What revolutions?  We rush to mistake the multiplication of little desires and little ful-fillments for change because we fear nothing ever changes.

412.

I am not unambitious.  I am just too ambitious for what *you* call ambitions.

413.

Sexiness dates.  Beauty, on the other hand, does well with a touch of the archaic:  it does not need us.

414.

Disease is whatever tries to turn us into itself.

415.

Telling your troubles will be a relief only if shame is one of them. But even in what seemed the most blameless afflictions, there it is.

416.

That my youth was youthless once plagued me. By now it is an advantage: I waste no time on nostalgia.

417.

What were you like back then? Better to look at the young than trust your memory.

418.

Am I the past? As a lake forgets the rain.

419.

I need to blame pain. If you did nothing to deserve it, there is no way I can avoid it. And if I'm the one in pain, better to blame myself than doubt I can escape by doing something right.

420.

If we remembered even a fraction of our million tiny plans, our whole lives would be regret at their failure.

421.

Some things should be fixed, others left broken.

422.

The truth is no excuse.

423.

That we're here seems a wonder; on the other hand, who would be wondering if we weren't?

424.

The hawkers of self-help tell you to simplify yourself to confidence, optimism, positive feeling. Every time you hear a knock it will be you, selling yourself to yourself.

425.

Opportunity is so frequent a visitor that it doesn't bother to knock. The real lost chances are there every day to be lost.

426.

If they say *it's unique* they want you to buy. If you think *I'm unique* you're trying to sell.

427.

The first quest or the first love is also the last. The second isn't.

428.

Over the door of hell it says *Abandon hope*. Also over the door of heaven.

429.

Others must suffer now lest our old suffering lose its meaning.

430.

If you cannot heal your wound, praise its faithfulness.

431.

What's the difference between provincialism, which unthinkingly takes its situation for everyone's, and cosmopolitanism, which is confident it has the right to?

432.

Whatever death, whatever nothingness you imagine, is impure, since imagination is there.

433.

I imagine god as someone I would not like, perhaps because I can only imagine him as someone who needs to be god.

434.

Does distance separate us? Our bodies? Words? We imagine somehow our minds blending. But our two thoughts laid next to each other would no more merge than socks.

435.

Truth is like the flu. I fight it off, but it changes in other bodies and returns in a form to which I am not immune.

436.
You can't smell what the guests smell.

437.
The worst thing about fools is that they are so gallingly sure we care what they think.

438.
Anger has been ready to be angry.

439.
In the most personal sense, injustice is not being known as we are. For a writer, therefore, the first injustice is language. But do not read my mind.

440.
Bitterness is a greater failure than failure.

441.
*Judge not lest ye also be judged,* it is said, but you will not have to wait for this retaliation: judging itself brings the pain of being judged. The wicked judge mistakes this for another crime of the accused and lengthens his sentence.

442.

The saddest thing about bitterness is that it still glistens with hope.

443.

When you suspect me of a sin I did not commit, I am innocent of those I did.

444.

More dangerous than the worst is the pretty good you can no longer tell from the best.

445.

When we hate everything what we really hate is not knowing what we really like.

446.

They imagine Death and Judgment together because to be judged perfectly is to disappear. Now that I think of it, it's not justice I want, but to be misunderstood on my own terms.

447.

In heaven, maybe, rigor: everything you have done looked at from a single perspective, and either praised or cut away. But for now you are a summer rental, passed through by vacationers who never meet to discuss what they shared.

448.

Perfection can have only one witness.

449.

Hasn't there, once or twice, been a little too much zeal in our reproof of children and friends for yielding to the temptations we ourselves find it most difficult to resist? We punish where we can least afford to sympathize. Of all the horrors of the daily news, it seems hardest to imagine the kind of cruelty that is intensified by the pain of its victims, but whenever we feel sympathy would weaken us, we are a little closer to the torturer.

450.

That the bookstores divide into romance and mystery suggests the two most powerful fantasies are someone to love and someone to blame.

451.

Patience is decisive indecision.

452.

We like believing the best because nothing needs to be done about it, and the worst, because nothing can.

453.

The mercy of a stone is in asking no mercy.

454.

What's thinking? You live in a grandly appointed house, but spend all your time rummaging in the attic for any little trinket you hadn't known was there.

455.

The days are exactly alike in that they repeat nothing exactly.

456.
This sentence is headed to the future, and past it, into the past.

457.
Blocking the supermarket aisles, the agéd. They have lost that sense, separate from sight and hearing, that someone is behind them, as if they were staring too intently into some faint fire.

458.
Is it an answer, the Silence, or a question?

459.
When I am trying to write I turn on music so I can hear what is keeping me from hearing.

460.
Opacity gives way. Transparency is the mystery.

461.

Truths are likenesses of other truths. So those who concentrate on finding them discover there are fewer really distinct truths than they'd expected. Some conclude that there is only one. The truth is: many truths find you, though only a few can be found.

462.

The sun sees nothing.

463.

Listen. But not too carefully, since what I'm saying is not exactly what I mean.

464.

It's easier to agree on the future than the past.

465.

Only half of writing is saying what you mean. The other half is preventing people from reading what they expected you to mean.

466.

Easy to criticize yourself, harder to agree with the criticism.

467.

What happens, it is asked, to all the promising young? They promise what *we* wanted; they become what *they* wanted.

468.

The things we cannot escape—mortality, desire, shame, loss—make us think we are all the same. The things we want—money, justice, fame—make us think we might be different.

469.

All work is the avoidance of harder work.

470.

For one who needs it, praise is pity.

471.

If you never do a thing you may regret later, later will never come. As Eve proved, shame is time.

472.

We invent a god to help us understand solitude. In time, we give him a wife, a son, pets, students. He seems kinder; we know him better. But then we need a new god.

473.

How terrible to know what we will one day think of all we are now. So we call that Heaven or Posterity and say we have to die to get there, which is not so far from the truth, since the knowing is a kind of death.

474.

If I knew how I would feel about things later, it would already be later.

475.

We have secrets from others. But our secrets have secrets from us.

476.

Some of my secrets everybody knows, but not that they are secrets.

477.

What a relief when you have finally maneuvered yourself into a position where anyone would agree the only thing left to do is tell the truth.

478.

The great liars are credulous; they have convinced themselves first of all.

479.

Tell the truth lest it become too true.

480.

The lessons of one decade become the innocence of the next.

481.

Our lives get complicated because complexity is so much simpler than simplicity.

482.

Much of what you learn from a book or a job or a love you understand only when you have left it.

483.

Even going back is going forward.

484.

How we struggle to articulate all we don't know, how we fear coming to the end of it.

485.

Happiness is gratitude in search of something to be owed to.

486.

There, all along, was what you wanted to say. But this is not what you wanted, is it, to have said it?

487.

Many gods reward, one punishes.

488.

They gave me most who took most gladly of my love.

489.

I'm sitting here bored, trying to understand.
No: trying to remember that everything is a
complete mystery.

490.

Birds are amazing, newspapers, stoves, friends.
All that happens is amazing, if you think about
it. All that doesn't happen is even more amaz-
ing, because there's so much more of it. Only
habit keeps us from seeing all this. Habit is
really amazing.

491.

It's unwise to think your life is too small for
you. And too wise to think it isn't.

492.

Writing a book is like doing a huge jigsaw
puzzle, unendurably slow at first, almost self-
propelled at the end. Actually, it's more like
doing a puzzle from a box in which several
puzzles have been mixed. Starting out, you
can't tell whether a piece belongs to the puzzle
at hand, or one you've already done, or will do
in ten years, or will never do.

493.

The future would be easier to wait for if we could be sure it wasn't already happening.

494.

Things fall of their own weightlessness.

495.

What happened to the years? How did I get this way? By being this way.

496.

Who, after all, can say *The life I lived was not my life?*

497.

I'm trying to hold it all in my head, Life, one swift, lifelong sentence, clause depending on clause, parenthesis within parenthesis, whose meaning will come together only with its very last word.

498.

What I hope for is more hope.

499.
To feel an end is to discover that there had been a beginning. A parenthesis closes that we hadn't realized was open).

500.
*All things in moderation,* wisdom says. And says last *Do not be too wise.*

## ACKNOWLEDGEMENTS

Many of these aphorisms have appeared in *Yale Review, Ontario Review, Press, Michigan Quarterly Review, Ploughshares, Poetry Daily* and *Best American Poetry 2001*.

Somehow the "Aphorisms" section of my local book-arama has disappeared between "Abs" and "Appetites, Abnormal." On the evidence of shelf space, anyway, a collection of cracks and oracles is several orders of magnitude less likely even than the slim volumes of poetry I'm usually guilty of, and I owe proportionately more to the friends, editors, and editor-friends whose kind words and pointed advice helped me to persist in what I was often tempted to regard more as a questionable habit than as a book in progress. Large thanks to Diane Boller, Gerald Costanzo, Diana Fuss, Laurence Goldstein, Robert Hass, Victoria Kahn, Don Lee, David Lehman, J.D. McClatchy, Paul Muldoon, Jeff Nunokawa, Joyce Carol Oates, Joanna Picciotto, Raymond Smith, Esther Schor, Chase Twichell, Don Selby, Edmund White, Renée & Theodore Weiss, and C. K. Williams.

This book was begun and completed with the timely assistance of 1993-1994 and 2001-2002 Artists Fellowships from the New Jersey State Council on the Arts.